How to set up a MacBook Air 2020

A step by step guide to your MacBook Air

Bernard Gates

copyright@2020

Introduction

Apple has surprised users with what they have done to the new MacBook Air. The new Air improves over the previous model in various ways. Let's look at some of them: first off, the 2020 version is now more powerful, thanks to the upgrades to the CPU, RAM and storage capacity. Specifically, you get dual or quad core processors with the M1 chip and up to 16GB of RAM depending on the model you decide to get. There are 3 models in the Air line up. The entry level has a dual core 10th generation intel core i3 processor, 256GB storage and 8GB of RAM and retails for $999. The mid-level model packs a 10th generation quad core intel i5 processor, 512GB, 8GB RAM and sells for $1,299. The high-end version has an intel core i7 processor, 16GB RAM, 2TB SSD and goes for $2,249.

Apple also decided to add the magic keyboard to the Air series which users would definitely prefer over the keyboard on the previous model.

The Air comes with a 13.3-inch screen, a 2,560x 1,600 Retina True Tone display, two thunderbolt 3 ports that offer transfer speeds of up to 40Gb/s and transmit up to 6k footage to a compatible monitor and a 3.5mm headphone jack. For connectivity, it has an 802.11ac Wi-Fi, and Bluetooth. The camera is a 720 pixels FaceTime HD webcam. The Air weighs about 2.8 pounds or 1.29kg and the has a size of 11.97x 8.36x 0.63 inches. As a result of the addition of new components, the Air weighs a bit more but you can still effortlessly lug it around. It's still Apple's lightest laptop.

The MacBook Air also incorporates a Touch ID fingerprint scanner that users can use to login to macOS and equally use for paying for stuff online via Apple pay.

The speakers on the MacBook Air can hold its own as it delivers clear and quality sound. It's great for playing audio and watching videos. Battery life is between 7 and 8 hours

The Apple MacBook Air comes with the same brushed finish and users can choose from Gold, Silver or space gray colors.

Table of Contents

Introduction 2

Chapter one: set up 9

    Setting up your new MacBook Air 9

    Moving stuff from a previously owned Mac to your new Mac Air 13

    Moving your data and stuff from PC to your new Mac Air 16

Chapter 2: creating an Apple ID on your Mac Air 19

    Using the Mac Music app to create an Apple ID 19

    Creating an Apple ID via the web 21

Chapter 3: Using the Dock 23

    Adding apps to the Dock 23

    Adding folders or files to the Dock 24

    Removing files, folders or apps from the Dock 24

    Organizing the Dock on your Mac Air 24

    Changing the Dock size on your Mac Air 25

    Changing the orientation of the Dock on your Mac 26

    Showing or hiding the Dock 26

    Hiding recent applications on the Dock 27

Chapter 4: The menu bar 28

    Removing widgets from the menu bar 28

    Changing the date and time from the menu bar 28

    Changing the Time zone manually 30

    Changing the look of the date and time Menu bar widget 31

    Rearranging Menu bar icons 33

Chapter 5: The Magic mouse 34

Changing the right-clicking, scroll direction and tracking speed of your mouse: 34

Changing the speed of double-clicking your mouse settings............ 35

Changing the scrolling speed setting of your mouse 36

Changing the gestures of your Magic Mouse.....................................37

Chapter 6: The trackpad... 40

Changing the speed of the tracking function..................................... 40

Speeding up or slowing down the scrolling function 41

Speeding up or slowing down double-clicking.................................. 43

Chapter 7: Right-clicking on your mouse or trackpad .. 44

Activating right-clicking for a Magic Mouse 44

Activating right-clicking for a Magic Trackpad or MacBook trackpad 45

Chapter 8: pairing your Mac with your Apple Watch (Auto Unlock) 47

Activating auto unlock on your Mac Air.. 47

Chapter 9: Apple pay 49

Setting up Apple Pay on your Mac Air: 49

Using Apple Pay on your Mac Air with Touch ID 52

Managing your Apple Pay cards on your Mac with Touch ID 53

Changing your default card 54

Removing a card.. 55

Managing your contact and shipping information 55

Managing your billing Address 56

Viewing recent transactions 57

Chapter 10: The finder 58

Launching a Finder Window 58

Customizing the Finder toolbar 59
Using quick look 61
Using the info button 62
Showing or hiding external or internal paraphernalia 63
Setting a new Finder Window default section 64
Using Tags 65
Creating Custom Tags 66
Customizing the Finder sidebar 67
Using Stacks in Finder 69
Using Gallery View in Finder 70
Viewing file metadata in Finder 71
Using Quick actions in Finder 73
Using Quick Look tools in Finder 75

Chapter 11: The Mac App Store 76
Downloading apps from the Mac app store 76

Chapter 12: Desktop background and screen saver 77
How to pick a built-in desktop image 77
Picking a dynamic desktop image 78
Using your own image as your background 80
Setting up rotating backgrounds 82
Setting up screen savers 84
Setting up hot corners 86

Chapter 13: messaging 88
Setting up iMessaging on your Mac 88
Setting up messages in iCloud in macOS 89

Chapter 14: mail 91

Setting up a mail account: 91

Setting how often Mail checks for new messages 91

Selecting Mail notification sounds 92

Adding a signature 93

Sending a new email 94

Replying to an email 95

Viewing and downloading email attachments 95

Locating specific email messages 96

Filtering email by unread 97

Marking an email as Unread 98

Deleting an email 99

Chapter 15: Safari 100

Visiting a website 100

Searching with the address bar 100

Bookmarking a website 101

Viewing all bookmarks 102

Removing Bookmarks 103

Adding a web page to your reading list 104

Viewing your reading list 104

Deleting items from your reading list 105

Enabling Private Browsing 106

Pinning Tabs 107

Setting the homepage 107

Sharing websites 109

Customizing Favorites in Safari 109

Organizing your Safari Favorites 109

6

Organizing your frequently visited sites in Safari 110

Deleting frequently visited sites 110

Accessing Siri suggestions in Safari in macOS Catalina 111

Chapter 16: Launch pad 112

Opening apps via launchpad on your Mac 112

Locating apps via Launchpad 112

Moving apps around in Launchpad 113

Sorting apps into folders 113

Deleting apps in Launchpad 114

Resetting Launchpad 115

Chapter 17: Siri 116

Enabling Siri on your Mac Air 116

Activating "Type to Siri" (for macOS High Sierra) 117

Typing a query to Siri (macOS High Sierra) 118

Using a keyboard shortcut to enable Siri 118

Using Siri with AirPods 119

Pinning Siri results to notifications center 119

Chapter 18: Spotlight 120

Accessing and using Spotlight 120

Customizing Spotlight search results 120

Hiding content from Spotlight search 121

Chapter 20: Screenshots 122

Taking screen shots on your Mac Air 122

Doing a Screen recording 122

Choosing a save location for screenshots and screen recordings ... 124

Setting a timer for screenshots and screen recordings 124

7

Showing the mouse pointer in screenshots 125
Editing a screenshot 125
Editing a screen recording 126

Chapter 21: Full screen mode 128

Entering full screen mode 128
Navigating around full screen mode 128
Exiting full-screen mode 129

Chapter one: set up

Setting up your new MacBook Air

So, you just purchased your MacBook Air and are about to set it up and get down to getting the most out of it. If you are a first timer or you just upgraded from a previous MacBook, the steps to setting it up are very simple and easy to follow. It's as simple as following the steps below:

- power it up by pushing the **Power button.**
- Next, choose a **language**
- Click **Continue**

- Next, choose your preferred **keyboard layout** and click **Continue**

- Choose a **Wi-Fi network.** In case you want to connect via other means, **click Other Network Options**
- If you selected Wi-Fi, key in your **password** and click **Continue**

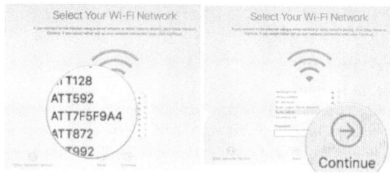

- Next, click **Don't transfer any information now** if you don't want move any data or stuff from another Mac or PC
- Click **Continue**

- Next, check or tick the box for **Enable Location Services on this Mac** if you want Apple to access your location and click **Continue**

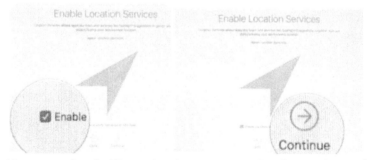

- Use your **Apple ID** to sign in to access Apple services. If you don't have one yet, it's possible to create one later
- Click **Continue** when you are done signing in

- **Agree** to terms and conditions
- **Agree** again to confirm

- Next, type a **Full name** for your computer
- Enter an **Account name**

- Key in a **password** for your Mac and enter a **Hint** to help you remember the password
- If you prefer to use your Apple ID to reset your Mac password, tick or check the box
- If you enabled location services, tick the box for **Set time zone based on current location**

11

- Click **Continue**
- Next, tick or check the box for **Turn on FileVault disk encryption** to encrypt your Mac's hard drive
- Tick or check the box **for Allow my iCloud account to unlock my disk** directly under the box for FileVault disk encryption
- Click **Continue**

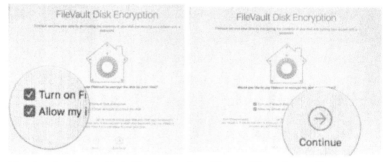

- Next, check or tick the box for **Store files from Documents and Desktop in iCloud**
- Click **Continue**

- Tick or check the box for **Enable Siri on this Mac**
- Click **Continue**

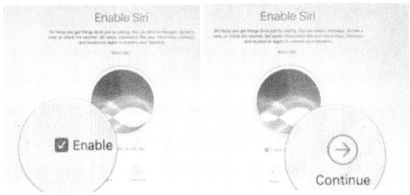

- When you get to this point, your Mac will continue with finishing up the settings that you have specified. You may be prompted to take some actions such as allowing, continuing or turn on certain settings to finish the process

Moving stuff from a previously owned Mac to your new Mac Air
In case you have an old Mac and just upgraded to a new one and want to move your data to the new one, there are several ways you can do this and there is a checklist to execute. Let's start with the checklist:

1. Make sure you have the latest software
2. Make sure your old Mac has a name
3. Both Macs must be connected to power sources
4. If you want to use cable instead of Wi-Fi, get the cable ready

Basically, you can move stuff from your old Mac to the new by a data cable or Wi-Fi. If you want to use a cable, you can use a Thunderbolt, FireWire or Ethernet cable. To transfer Data to your new Mac from the old, follow the steps below:

- If you are using cable, connect it from the old Mac to the new and if you are using Wi-Fi, ensure that both computers are connected to the same network
- On your new Mac, open a **Finder window** by clicking on the finder icon from the Dock
- Next, click on **Applications** from the sidebar

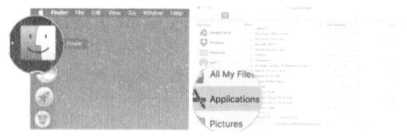

- Click the **Utilities folder** twice in quick succession
- Do the same as above for the **Migration Assistant** folder

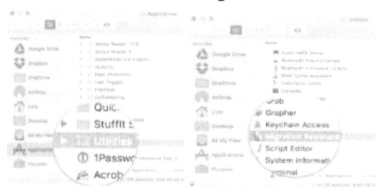

- Click **Continue**
- Key in your **administrator password** if required
- Click **OK**

14

- Select **From a Mac** when you view the screen that specifies transfer Options
- Click **Continue**

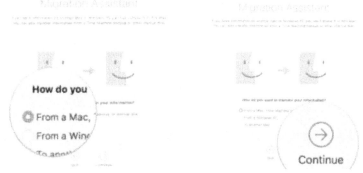

- Repeat the same steps as above on your **old Mac** from opening the finder window to clicking OK after typing your administrator's password
- Go back to the new Mac and choose your old Mac
- Click **Continue.** You should view a **security code** displayed on the screen

- Revert to the old Mac and make sure that it has the same **security code** displayed as on the screen of the new Mac

15

- Click **Continue**

- From your new Mac, select the data including **settings, files, apps** and any other stuff you want to move to the new Mac
- Click **Continue**

- At this point, the process of transferring the data from your old mac to the new would commence. You may have to be a bit patient based on the amount of stuff you are moving.

Moving your data and stuff from PC to your new Mac Air

If you are new to Apple and want to transfer you stuff or data from an old PC, there are things you must know and steps to take.

1. First off, you need to have an Apple utility called the migration software.
2. You would also need specific software based on what MacOS or OS X you are transferring to.
3. You have to download the Migration assistant software to your PC

16

4. Your windows PC must be running windows 7,8, or 10 and the stuff that eventually gets moved has a lot to do with the windows version your PC is running and the programs that created your data.
5. Your PC and Mac must be running the Migration Assistant
6. Your PC and Mac must be on the same network so they can be connected and communicate

Before you start:

- Make sure you have the administrative username and password you use on the PC
- The PC and Mac must be on the same Wi-Fi or Ethernet network
- Execute a drive performance check before you run the Migration Assistant. To do this, follow the steps below:
    1. From your PC, click **Start**
    2. Next, click **Run**
    3. In the Run window, type **cmd**
    4. **Press Enter**
    5. Next, in the command window, type **chkdsk**
    6. Press **Enter**

To move your stuff and information from your PC to Mac, follow the steps below:

- Tether your PC and Mac via Wi-Fi or Ethernet. Ensure that both are on the same network
- Open a new **Finder window** on your Mac
- From the sidebar, click on **Applications**
- Click twice on the **Utilities folder** in quick succession
- Next, click on the **Migration Assistant**
- Click **Continue**
- On the transfer screen or display, click **From a PC** when prompted to select how to transfer your information
- Click **Continue**

- If you have downloaded the **Migration Assistant** and installed it on your PC, open it. You should view a **security code** on your screen
- Check to confirm it's the same code you are viewing on your Mac
- Next, specify the files, folders and settings you want to move from your PC to Mac and click **Continue**

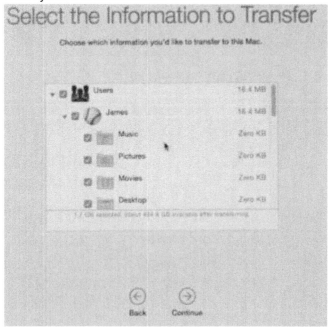

18

Chapter 2: creating an Apple ID on your Mac Air

Your Apple ID is very handy for accessing all Apple products and apps and services such as iCloud, Apple Pay, iTunes and purchasing stuff from the Apple app store. if you are new to Apple and don't have an Apple ID yet, there are two ways you can use to get one or sign up. Select one from below:

Using the Mac Music app to create an Apple ID

- Open the **Music app** from your **Dock or Finder**
- From the **toolbar**, click **Account**
- From the pull-down menu, select **Sign in**

- Click **Create New Apple ID**
- On the **Create Apple ID** page, enter your **personal data** which would include **email** and **password** and verify your **password** in the box provided for that purpose
- Agree to terms and conditions by ticking or checking the box
- Click **Continue**

19

- Enter your personal information or data such as **first name, last name** and **birthday** and click Continue

- Next, add your payment data which include: **your payment method, number, expiration date, security code, billing name and address**
- Click **Continue**

- Specify if you prefer to use **text or a phone call** for identity verification
- Next, add your phone number and click **Continue**

- Key in the **verification code** sent to you via text or phone call
- Click **Verify**
- Key in the **code** received via email and click **verify**
- You are done

Creating an Apple ID via the web

- Go to **applied.apple.com**
- At the bottom, **click Create Your Apple ID**
- Provide the needed information. Note that the **email** and **password** you enter would be your **Apple ID**
- Click **Continue** at page bottom. When you do this, you would get an email which would contain **a verification code**
- Next enter the **code** contained in the mail. It should be 6 digits
- Click **Continue**

21

- With this, you have completed then process. You can now add credit cards to purchase apps and iTunes content, add a billing or shipping address etc

Chapter 3: Using the Dock

The Dock is a small panel positioned at bottom of the screen of your Mac Air. It contains the apps shortcuts, files, folders and functions that you may have to use frequently. It's possible for you to play around with the dock settings and make adjustments to its position and the position of some of the apps shortcut and functions within the dock. In this chapter, you would learn how to get around and manipulate the Dock.

Adding apps to the Dock
- From the **Dock**, open a **Finder Window**
- Next, in the **sidebar**, click **Applications**

- Choose an **app** and move or drag to the **Dock**
- When the **app** is positioned over the **Dock**, let go of it

- In case you want to keep an app in the Dock permanently, right-click on the app icon in your Dock, select **Options** from the **drop-down menu** and click on **Keep in Dock**

Adding folders or files to the Dock

If you want to add files and/or folders to your dock, there is a position for them which is the far right. To add files or folders, follow the steps below:

- Open a **Finder Window** from your **Dock**
- Choose a **file or folder** from its position and move it to the right side of your **Dock**
- While the **folder or file** is positioned over the **Dock**, let go of it

Removing files, folders or apps from the Dock

When or if you decide you don't, want an app, file or folder anymore on your dock, or you want to remove a file, folder or app to make room for another, follow the steps below:

- Pick an **app, folder or file** and move it out from the **Dock**
- When you have it positioned over the **desktop**, the word Remove appears over the **app, folder or file**
- If you let go of the **app, folder or file**, it would automatically be removed from the **Dock**

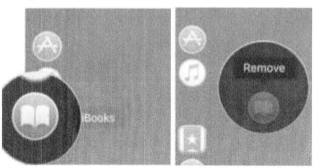

Organizing the Dock on your Mac Air

There are various options you have for organizing or rearranging the apps, files or folders in your Dock based on your preference. You can do an alphabetical order, a color coordinated arrangement etc.

- Choose a **folder, file** or an **app** from the **Dock**
- Move it to a new position in the **Dock**

24

- While it hovers over the new position where you want it to be, let go of the **folder, file** or **app**

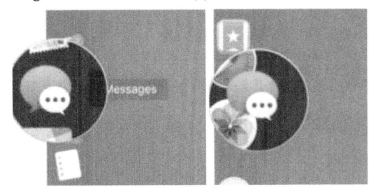

Changing the Dock size on your Mac Air
- From upper left corner of your screen, click the **Apple icon**
- Next, choose or select **System Preferences** from the drop-down menu

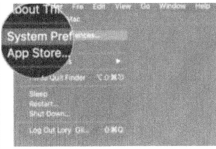

- Select or click **Dock**
- Move the **Size** control slider to left or right to increase or reduce the size of the Dock

25

- check or tick the box for **Magnification** to activate an animation that increases the size of the items in the **Dock** that your cursor hovers over
- next, move or drag the **slider** that controls **Magnification** to the left or right to increase or reduce how large the icons become when the cursor hovers over them

Changing the orientation of the Dock on your Mac

If you don't like the default position of the Dock, you can move it to a preferred position which could be the right or left side of the screen by following the steps below:

- from upper left of the screen, click on the **Apple icon**
- click **System Preferences** from the drop-down menu
- click on **Dock**
- choose from between **Left, Bottom** or **Right** to change the Dock position

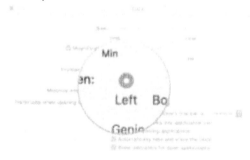

Showing or hiding the Dock

If you don't want the dock visible unless you need it, follow the steps below:

26

- from upper left of screen, click the **Apple icon**
- click **System Preferences** from the **drop-down menu**
- click on **Dock**
- check or tick the box for **Automatically hide and show the Dock**

Hiding recent applications on the Dock

- launch or access **System Preferences** from your **Dock** or **Applications folder**
- click **Dock**

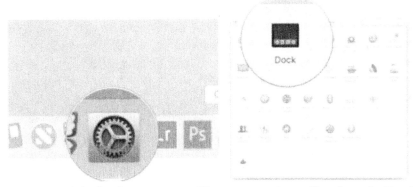

- next, tick the box next to **Show recent applications in Dock** so that the check disappears since it's on by default

Chapter 4: The menu bar

The menu bar is situated at the top of the screen of the screen and it contains useful shortcuts to the most important features you would be referring to or making use of. On the menu bar, you find things like the Apple menu, the app menu, the system status menu, spotlight, Siri and the notification center. In this chapter, you would learn the various options and settings available and how to navigate around the menu bar

Removing widgets from the menu bar
- **Right-click** on the **widget** in the **Menu bar**
- choose **Open Preferences**
- uncheck the box for **Show in Menu bar**

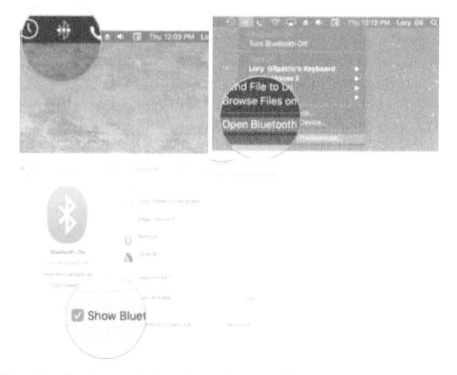

Changing the date and time from the menu bar
- from the upper right corner of the **menu bar**, click on the **date and time**
- next, click on **Open Date & Time Preferences**

28

- click the **Date & Time** tab
- click the **lock** to effect make your adjustments
- Key in your administrator password and click **unlock**

- Uncheck the box for **Set Date and Time automatically**
- Set a new **Date**
- Set a new **Time**

29

Changing the Time zone manually

- From upper right of your screen, click on the **date and time** in the **menu bar**
- Click on **Open Date & Time Preferences**
- Click on the **Time Zone** tab
- Click the **lock** to change settings
- Type your administrator password and click **Unlock**

30

- Uncheck the box for **Set time zone automatically using current location**
- Click on a **new region**

Changing the look of the date and time Menu bar widget
- From upper right of screen, click on **date and time** in the menu bar
- Click on Open **Date & Time Preferences**
- Click the **clock** Tab
- Click the **lock** to make changes
- Type your administrator password and click **Unlock**

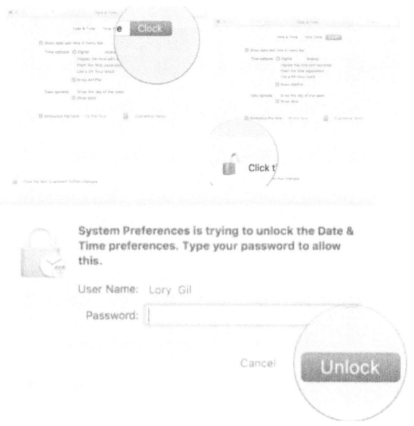

- Click **Digital** or **Analog** to change the clock appearance
- Check or tick the box for **Show the day of the week**
- Check or tick the box for **Show date**

Rearranging Menu bar icons
- Press and hold the **command key** on your keyboard
- Next, click on the **icon** to be moved while retaining your hold on the command key

- Move the **icon** to its new location
- Release the **mouse** and **command key** to allow the icon take its new position

Chapter 5: The Magic mouse

Whatever be your preference when it comes to using a mouse, you can adjust the settings of the magic mouse on your Mac to that which gives you the best functionality for better and faster productivity. MacOS allows you to change the default mouse setting. Find how below:

Changing the right-clicking, scroll direction and tracking speed of your mouse:

- From the upper left corner of your screen, click the **Apple icon**
- Click **System Preferences** from the **dropdown menu**

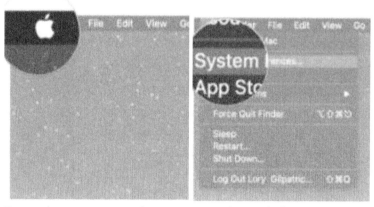

- From the system preferences window, click on **Mouse**
- Next, select **Point & Click**
- Check the box for **Scrolling direction: natural** to make the mouse scroll in the same direction that your finger moves
- Check the box for **Secondary click** to enable right-clicking

- Click the **arrow** under **Secondary Click** to select if you use the mouse's right or left side to enable secondary clicking
- Move or drag the **Tracking Speed slider** left or right increase or reduce the speed at which the mouse pointer moves across the screen

Changing the speed of double-clicking your mouse settings

- Click the **Apple icon** at screen upper left
- Select or click **System Preference** from the **dropdown menu**

- Click **Accessibility** in the System Preferences window
- Navigate down and select **Mouse & Trackpad** from the menu on the left side of the Accessibility window
- Move or drag the **Double-click speed slider** to the right or left to increase or reduce how fast the mouse must be clicked to enable the double-click feature

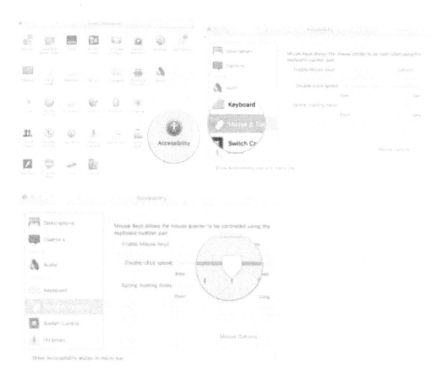

- Next, check the box for **Spring-Loading delay** to activate the feature that launches a folder when you hover over it with a file
- Drag the **Spring-loading delay slider** right or left to specify how long you must hover over a folder containing a file before it opens

Changing the scrolling speed setting of your mouse
- From upper-left corner of your screen, click the **Apple icon**
- Next, click **System Preferences** from the dropdown menu
- Click Accessibility while within the System Preferences window

36

- Next, click **Mouse Options**
- Use the **Scrolling Speed Slider** to specify how fast or slow you can scroll by dragging the slider left or right
- When you are satisfied, click **OK** to exit

Changing the gestures of your Magic Mouse
- From upper left corner of your screen, click the **Apple icon**
- Choose System preferences from the **dropdown menu**
- While still in the System Preferences window, click **Mouse**
- Select **point & Click**
- Check the box for **Smart Zoom** to activate the ability to double-tap the magic mouse to zoom in a window
- Next, click on **More Gestures**
- Check or tick the box for **Swipe between pages** to use your finger to swipe or scroll left and right on the magic mouse
- At this point, click the **arrow** under Swipe between pages to specify if you scroll left and right using one finger, or swipe left and right using two fingers or do the same alternating between one or two fingers

37

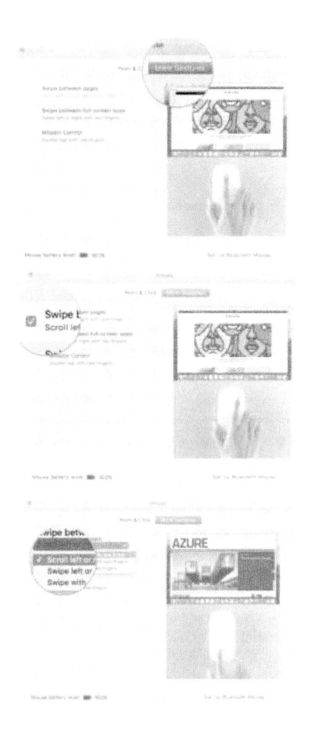

- Check or tick the box for **Swipe between full-screen apps** to activate the capacity to swipe left or right to switch from one full screen to another
- Check or tick the box for **Mission Control** to launch the capacity to call up mission control by tapping the Magic Mouse

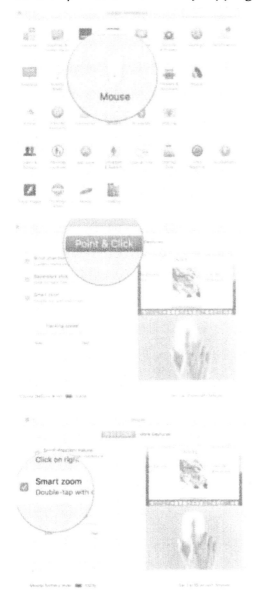

Chapter 6: The trackpad

If you prefer the arrow pointer on the screen to be lightming fast or as slow as possible so that you can keep track of its movement on the screen, there are such settings that you can use to customize the functions of your trackpad.

Changing the speed of the tracking function

- From upper left corner of your screen, click the **Apple icon**
- From the dropdown menu, select **System preferences**

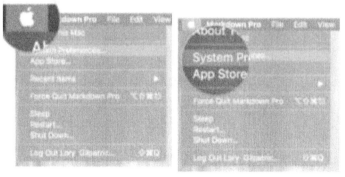

- Click on **Trackpad**
- Next, click on **Point & Click**

40

- To speed up or slow down the cursor speed, move the **tracking speed slider** to the right or left based on your preference
- Next, move the **Click pressure slider** to the right or left as the case may be to make the click pressure more firm or lighter

- Uncheck or untick the box for Silent clicking if you don't want the trackpad clicking sound
- Uncheck or untick the box for Force Click and haptic feedback if you prefer not to have haptic feedback when you force click your trackpad

 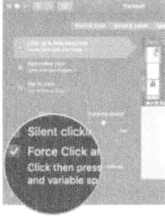

Speeding up or slowing down the scrolling function
- From upper left corner, click the **Apple icon**
- From the dropdown menu, select **System preferences**
- Next, click **Accessibility**

41

- Navigate down and click **Pointer Controls** from the list

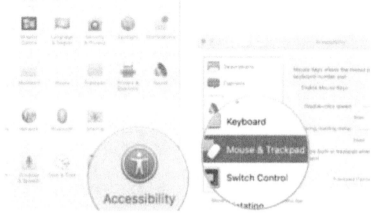

- Click on **Trackpad Options**
- To speed up or slow down the scrolling speed, move the **Scrolling speed Slider** to right or left based on your preference

42

Speeding up or slowing down double-clicking
- From upper left corner of your screen, click the **Apple icon**
- From the dropdown menu, click **System Preferences**
- Click on **Accessibility**
- Navigate down and click **Pointer Controls**

- To speed up or slow down the double-clicking speed, move the **Double-click speed slider** to right or left based on your preference

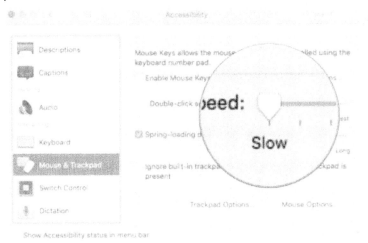

43

Chapter 7: Right-clicking on your mouse or trackpad

Your Mac Air isn't set up like any laptop running the windows system especially as regards the way a mouse or trackpad works on any windows device. All Mac devices do not come with a mouse or trackpad that has a normal right mouse button as do windows devices but it doesn't mean you can't access the right-clicking function; it only means you have to learn the Apple way of doing it and it also means you have to enable the right-clicking function. Find how to do so below:

By default, pressing and holding down the Control key on your Mac Air keyboard and pressing your primary mouse or trackpad button would launch a shortcut or menu and grant a windows device kind of access that windows users are used to seeing from a simple right -click of their mouse but to alter the settings of your Mac simulate the windows device kind of experience, follow the steps below:

Activating right-clicking for a Magic Mouse

- From upper left corner of your Mac screen, click the **Apple button** or do so from the **Dock** at screen bottom
- Click **System preferences**
- Click **Mouse**

- Next, click the **checkbox** next to **Secondary click** and select between "click on the right side" or "click on the left side" based on your preference

44

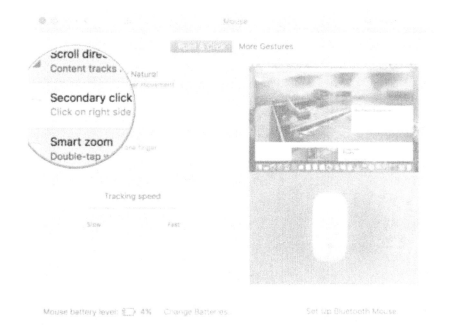

Activating right-clicking for a Magic Trackpad or MacBook trackpad

- From upper left corner of your screen, click the **Apple button** and then from the dropdown menu, click **System preferences** or from the **Dock**, launch **System Preferences**
- Next, click on the **Trackpad** icon

45

- Go to the **Point and Click** tab
- Select the **checkbox** next to **Secondary click**

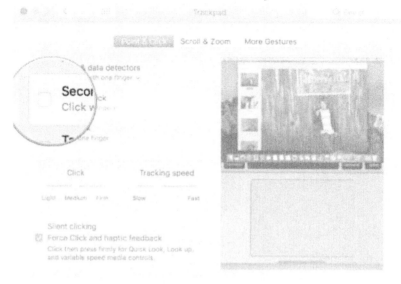

Chapter 8: pairing your Mac with your Apple Watch (Auto Unlock)

Apple has built in a cross functionality in its devices and this makes it possible for them to be used in other capacities such as information or data exchange, sharing or back up. It also possible for users that have multiple Apple devices to use one to unlock the other by means of pairing. This is true of the Apple watch and your Mac. If you have the right Mac and Apple watch, and you follow the steps properly, then unlocking your Mac is as easy as just sitting down in front of your Mac. However, as easy as it sounds, there is a checklist of requirements that you must make execute before this is possible. Find this checklist below:

1. You must have the right Apple watch and Mac, typically a mid-2013 and later Mac and any Apple watch
2. An updated operating system on both devices. For your Mac, you need at least, MacOS sierra or later. For your Apple watch, watchOS 3 or later
3. Two factor authentication for your iCloud account
4. Your Mac Air Apple watch must be signed in to the same iCloud account using the same Apple ID
5. Both devices must have a passcode
6. Your Mac Air must have Wi-Fi and Bluetooth activated
7. Your Apple watch must be on and unlocked

Activating auto unlock on your Mac Air

- Click the **Apple icon** at upper left corner of your screen
- From the drop-down menu, click **System Preferences**

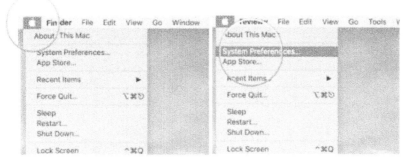

- Next, click on **Security & Privacy**

47

- Click **General**
- Check or tick the box **to Use your Apple watch to unlock apps and your Mac**

Chapter 9: Apple pay

Apple Pay is a payment solution devised by Apple to enable users to find and pay for stuff online. Apple has gone to great lengths to make sure it's a safe and secure system that Apple users can comfortably use at any time. The good news is, no matter what Apple device you are using, you can still set up and make use of Apple pay. Follow the guide below to set up Apple pay on your Mac Air

Setting up Apple Pay on your Mac Air:
- On your Mac, launch **Safari**
- From upper left screen corner, click on **Safari**
- Next, click **System Preferences**

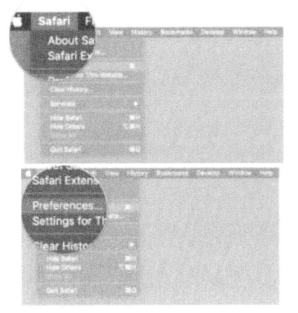

- Click the **Privacy** tab
- Check or tick the box close to **Apple Pay and Apple Card** to authorize websites to present you with the payment option

49

If your Mac Air is a Touch ID version, and you didn't set Apple Pay during the initial set up of your Mac Air, follow the guide below to set up and add your credit card:

- Go to **System Preferences**
- Click on **Wallet & Apple Pay**

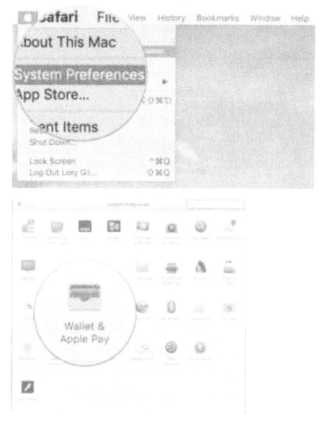

- Click on the **Add Card** button to add a new credit or debit card as the case may be

50

- Next, place your card in front of your **iSight** camera for it to automatically read or pick your card number or you can elect to enter the number **manually**

- after this, click **Next** to verify your card number
- Next, verify the card's expiration date and key in your three-number **security code**
- Click **Next**

- Click **Accept** to agree to your card issuer's terms and conditions
- Next, select a **verification method** to verify your card's setup
- Click **Next**

- Type in the **verification code** sent to you through your preferred method
- Click **Next**

Using Apple Pay on your Mac Air with Touch ID
- Go to **Safari** on your iPhone or iPad
- Browse a **participating retailer website** that allows Apple Pay
- Find your way to the **checkout process**
- Next, tap **Checkout with Apple Pay**
- Tap **Pay with Apple Pay**
- Confirm your **contact data** to verify that your shipping and billing address are the right ones
- Finally, place your Touch ID registered finger on the **Touch ID button** to affirm that you want to pay with Apple Pay

In case you have a Mac Air without Touch ID, follow the guide below:

- Launch Safari on your computer
- Browse a **participating retailer website** that allows Apple Pay
- Find your way to the **checkout process**
- Next, tap **Checkout with Apple Pay**
- Tap **Pay with Apple Pay**
- Confirm your **contact data** to verify that your shipping and billing address are the right ones
- Next, pick your **iPhone** or raise up the wrist on which you are wearing your **Apple watch**
- Finally, place your **Touch ID registered finger** on the Home button of your iPhone with Touch ID or press twice the **side**

52

button if you have a device with Face ID or press the **side button** if you have an Apple watch to pay for your purchase

Managing your Apple Pay cards on your Mac with Touch ID
- Launch **System preferences** on your Mac
- Click **Wallet & Apple Pay**

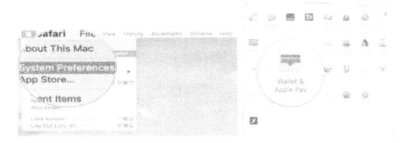

53

- Select a card from the side bar to view its data or information

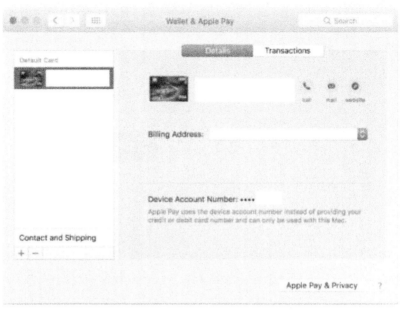

Changing your default card
- Go to **System Preferences** on your Touch ID enabled Mac Air
- Click **Wallet & Apple Pay**

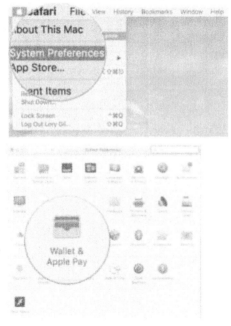

- From the bottom of the screen choose the card you want to use as your default card from the dropdown menu

Removing a card
- Go to **System Preferences** on your Mac Air with Touch ID
- Click on **Wallet & Apple Pay**

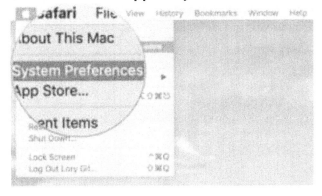

- **Choose** the card you want to delete from the side bar
- Next, press the – (delete) button at the sidebar bottom
- Finally, affirm that you wish to delete or remove the card

Managing your contact and shipping information
- Go to **System Preferences** on your Mac with Touch ID
- Click on **Wallet & Apple Pay**
- Click on the **contact and shipping information** at the sidebar bottom

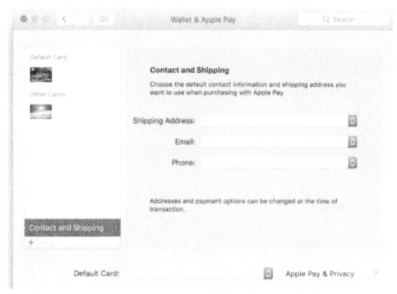

- Select the option you wish to make changes to from its dropdown menu. You can equally add a new address, email or phone number

Managing your billing Address
- Go to **System Preferences** on your Mac Air with Touch ID
- Click **Wallet & Apple Pay**
- Choose the card you want from the sidebar
- From the dropdown menu under the **Billing Address,** select **Add a new billing Address**

Viewing recent transactions
- Go to **System Preferences** on your Mac with Touch ID
- Click on **Wallet & Apple Pay**

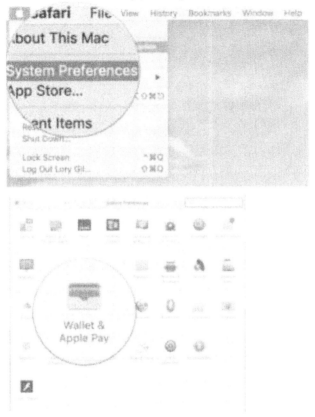

- Choose the **card** from the **sidebar**
- Next, click on **Transactions** at screen top

Chapter 10: The finder

You can liken the Finder on your Mac Air to an easy to use search function to help you quickly locate files, apps and downloads. A lot of stuff can be found or located in the finder. To learn how to make use of the finder, follow the guide below:

Launching a Finder Window

- Click on your desktop
- In the menu bar, click **File** and select **New Finder Window**

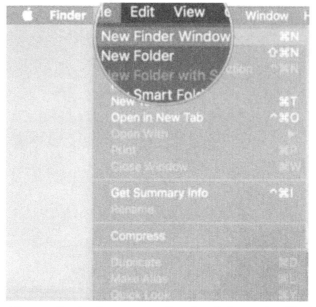

- Alternatively, from your **Dock,** click on the Finder icon

- A third way you can use to launch the finder is to select the keyboard and press 'Command-N'

Customizing the Finder toolbar
- Launch a Finder window
- While in the toolbar, Right-, control-, or use two fingers to click on the toolbar

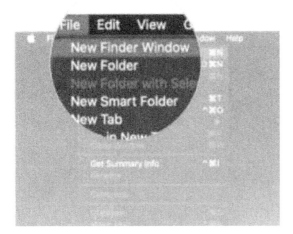

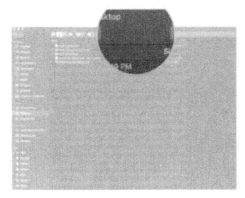

- Click Customize Toolbar
- Next, click on and drag different tools into the bar

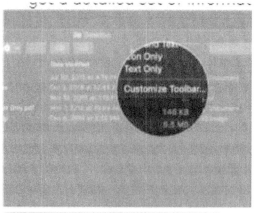

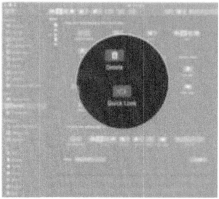

- Click **Done** when you are done adding all your preferred tools to the toolbar

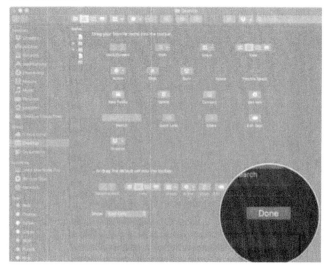

60

Using quick look

- Launch a new **Finder Window**
- Locate the file you want to use **Quick Look** to view and click on it just once

- On the **Finder toolbar,** click the **Quick Look** button or tap the space bar on your keyboard

Using the info button

- Launch a new **Finder Window**
- Click on any **item** you want to get information about

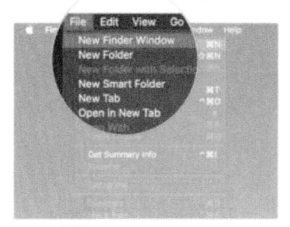

- Next, click the **info** button

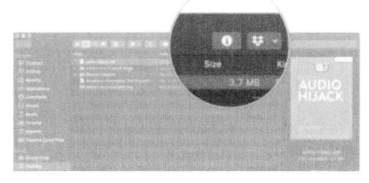

62

Showing or hiding external or internal paraphernalia

- While in Finder, click on **Finder** in the menu bar and choose Preferences
- Click **General**

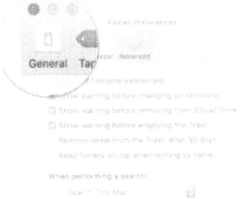

- Next, tick the boxes of the items you want displayed on the desktop

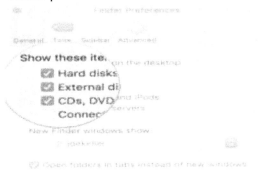

63

Setting a new Finder Window default section

- While in finder, click on **Finder** in the menu bar and click **Preferences**
- Click General

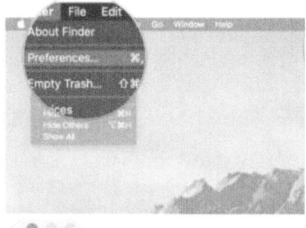

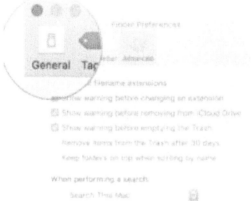

- From the dropdown menu, click on the folder or storage device
- If you do not see you selected section, select **Other**

64

Using Tags

- While in Finder, click on Finder in menu bar and click Preferences
- Click Tags

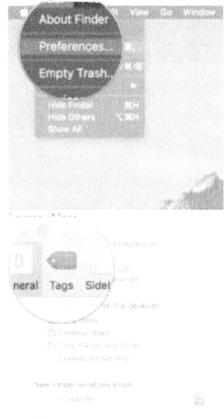

- Tick the **boxes** next to your tags to choose the tags that are shown in your **Finder sidebar**
- **Move or drag** a favorite tag to the **Tags tab bottom** to make it available for quick access in Finder menus

Creating Custom Tags

- While in Finder, click on **Finder** in the menu bar and choose Preferences
- Click **Tags**

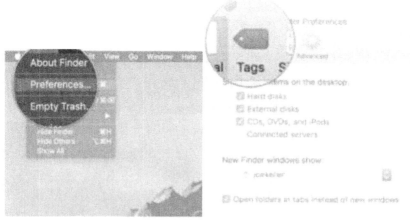

- From below the tags list, click the + button
- Next, type a **name** for your tag

- Assign your tag a color by clicking the **circle** next to it

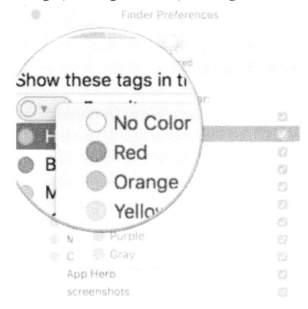

Customizing the Finder sidebar
- While in **Finder,** click on **Finder** in the menu bar and choose **Preferences**
- Click **Sidebar**

67

- Tick the boxes next to the items you want to view in your Finder's sidebar

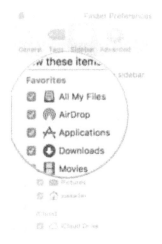

68

Using Stacks in Finder
- From your desktop, click **View** in the menu bar. Make sure that the foreground is clear of apps
- Click **Use Stacks**

- Control-click, right-click or two-finger click on your desktop
- Hover the mouse cursor over Group Stacks By and select from **Kind, Date Last Opened, Date Added, Date Modified, Date Created** and **Tags**

Using Gallery View in Finder
- From the Dock, click on the Finder icon to launch a new Finder window
- Go to the folder or section you want to view

- Next, click the Gallery View button to the extreme right side of the view selection buttons on the finder window

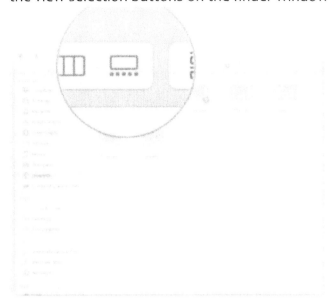

Viewing file metadata in Finder
- Launch a new Finder window by clicking on the **Finder** icon from your **Dock**
- Select the **view** you prefer to use

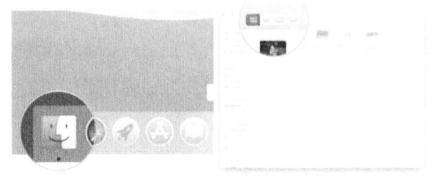

- Click on the **file** whose information you want to use
- From the menu bar, click **View**

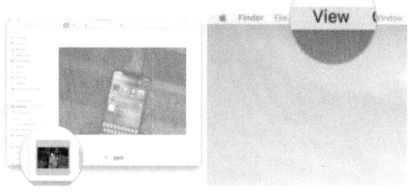

- Click **Show Preview**
- Click **Show More** in the Preview pane to view additional metadata

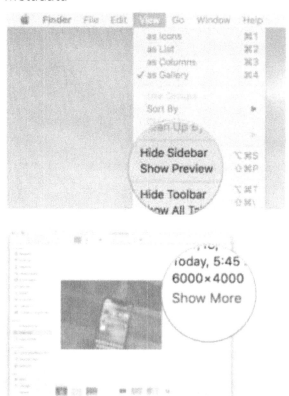

72

Using Quick actions in Finder

- Launch a new **Finder Window** by clicking on the **Finder** icon from your **Dock**
- Select the **view** you wish to make use of

- Click the **file** or **files** for which you want to do a quick action
- Click **View** from the menu bar

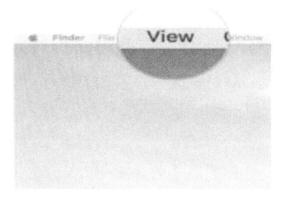

- Click **Show Preview**
- Select an **action** available from the **Preview Pane bottom** to carry it out on the selected file or files

- Click **More** in case you want to be able to locate other actions you want to carry out on the selected file or files

Using Quick Look tools in Finder
- Launch a new Finder window from your Dock
- Select the view you wish to use

- Select the file you want to use with **Quick Look**
- Next, tap the **space bar** on the keyboard to call up **Quick Look**
- Click the **action** button to execute action on the file. You can choose to **markup, rotate** or **trim** the file based on your preferences

Chapter 11: The Mac App Store

Your Mac Air comes with an app store that makes it possible for you to have access to a lot of additional apps that you could purchase or get for free. Based on what you are looking for, there are utility apps, productivity apps, games and a whole lot more. The Mac app store is safe, secure and user friendly.

Downloading apps from the Mac app store

- Launch the **App store** either from the **Dock, Launch pad** or via **spotlight**
- Browse through and locate an **app** you are interested in. there are featured apps and other app categories
- When you have found what you are looking for, click **Get** or click the **price** to download it (incase it's a paid app) by clicking **Get,** the button turns green and would display **Install.** If it's a paid app, it would display **Buy App**
- You may be asked to provide your **Apple ID** and **password** for the download to begin

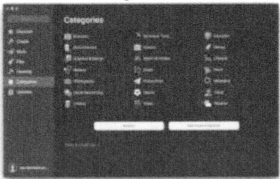

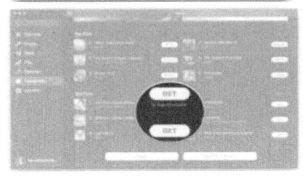

Chapter 12: Desktop background and screen saver

You can give a personal touch to your Mac Air by changing the default or pre-loaded images to an image or picture of your choice from your own collection. If you are interested in doing this, follow the guide or steps below:

How to pick a built-in desktop image

- Open **System Preferences** from the **Dock** or click the **Apple button** at top left of screen. you can equally right-click on the desktop image you wish to change and click Change Desktop Background
- Next, click **Desktop & Screen Saver**
- Choose **the Desktop tab**

- Click **Desktop Pictures** from under the Apple menu in the sidebar
- Next, click a **desktop image** under Desktop pictures

Picking a dynamic desktop image
- Go to **System Preferences** from **Dock** or click the **Apple button** at top left of screen
- Click **Desktop & Screen saver**
- Choose the **Desktop tab**

- Click **Desktop Pictures** under the **Apple menu** in the sidebar
- Next, click a **desktop image** under the **Dynamic Desktop** or **Light and Dark** Desktop section

Using your own image as your background
- Go to **System Preferences**
- Click **Desktop & Screen Saver**
- Select the **Desktop tab**

- Click the **+** button at sidebar bottom
- Click the **folder** that contains the image you want to use

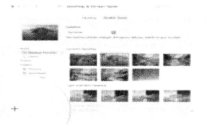

- Click **Choose**
- Click on your **chosen folder** in the sidebar
- Select an **image** from it

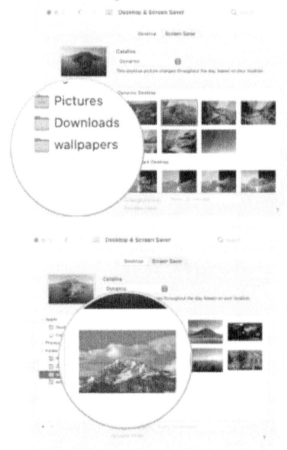

Setting up rotating backgrounds
- Go to **System Preferences**

82

- Click the **Desktop & Screen Saver**
- Select the **Desktop tab**

- Click on the **folder** you want to take wallpapers from
- Tick the box next to **Change picture**
- **Specify a duration** for the wallpaper to change\

Setting up screen savers
- Go to **System Preferences**
- Click **Desktop & Screen Saver**
- Click the **Screen Saver tab**

84

- Select your preferred **screen saver style**
- **Specify the source** you want to use for your screen saver from the **Source** dropdown menu

- Select **when** the screen saver should begin
- Toggle where to **Show with clock**
- Decide if you want a **random screen saver**

Setting up hot corners
- Go to **System Preferences**
- Click **Desktop & Screen Saver**

- Click the **screen Saver tab**

- Click **Hot Corners**
- Click the **associated dropdown menu** of the corner you want to customize
- Select the **action** to execute when using that Hot Corner
- When you are done, click **OK**

Chapter 13: messaging

Stay in touch with family, friends, colleagues or co-workers or even your boss with the messaging function of your Mac Air. You can use different messaging media such as iMessage and SMS to do this. It's very simple and straightforward but you have to set it up first especially if you are new to Apple or Mac.

Setting up iMessaging on your Mac

- Open the **Messages app** from your **Applications, Dock** or **desktop**. If the app does not automatically log you in, you have to enter your **Apple ID email** and **password**
- From the menu bar, click **Messages**
- Next, click **preferences**
- Click on the **iMessage** tab

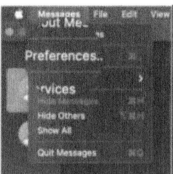

- Specify the **phone number** and **email** with which you can be reached

- Select the **phone number** or **email** people would view when you start a new conversation

Setting up messages in iCloud in macOS

- Launch **Messages** using your **desktop, Dock** or **Applications** folder
- In the **menu bar**, click **Messages**
- Click **Preferences**
- Click the **iMessage** tab

89

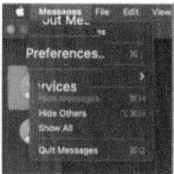

- Tick the box next to **Enable Messages on iCloud**
- Click **Sync Now** to begin the sync

Chapter 14: mail

You can use the mail app on your Mac to access all your mail accounts and do a whole lot of productive stuff. Here's how to start:

Setting up a mail account:
- Open the mail app from the Dock or using Finder
- Depending on the type of mail you use, click your email provider. If you can't view your provider in the options, click **Other Mail Account**
- Click **Continue**
- Enter your **email address** and **password**
- Click the **checkmark** next to each app you would like to use with the **account** you have selected
- Click **Done**

Setting how often Mail checks for new messages
- Open **Mail**

- Click **Mail** from menu bar at screen top left
- Click **preferences**
- Click **General** tab
- Click the **dropdown menu** next to **Check for new messages**
- Select a frequency

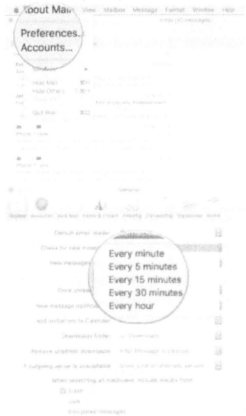

Selecting Mail notification sounds
- Open **Mail**
- Click **Mail** in menu bar at upper left of screen
- Click **Preference**
- Click the **General tab**
- Click the **dropdown menu** next to **New messages sound**
- Select or click a preferred **sound**

92

Adding a signature

- Open **Mail**
- Click **Mail** in menu bar at top left of screen
- Click **Preferences**
- Click the **Signatures** tab

93

- Click an **account** to add a signature to
- Click the **+ button** at lower center of window
- Type the **signature** in window at far right
- Click the **center window** to change the signature name
- Click the **dropdown menu** next to **Choose signature**
- Click an **option**

Sending a new email
- Open **Mail** from Dock or Finder
- Click **Compose**
- Type the **mail address** of the intended recipient or recipients as the case may be
- Enter a **Subject**
- Type the **email message or body**

94

- Click **Send button** at top left of the window

Replying to an email
- Open **Mail**
- Select the **mail** to which you would like to respond
- Click the **Reply button.** you have the option of replying to more than one mail, in which case, you click the **Reply All button.** if you want to share the mail with others, click the button for **Forward**

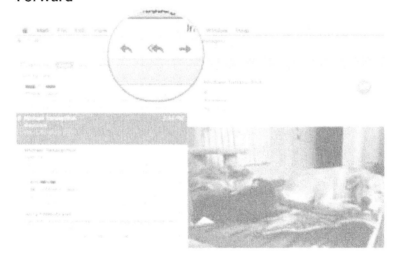

Viewing and downloading email attachments
- Open **Mail**
- Access the **email** that contains the **attachment**
- Click on a document in the body of the email twice to open and view it
- Mouse over the **white area** next to **To** and **From**

- Click on the **downward arrow** next to the number on the little **number** that shows up
- Click the **name** of the file attached
- Select a **destination** or **location** to save the attached file and click **Save**

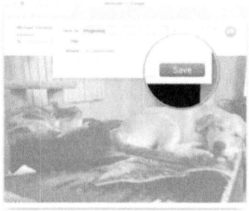

Locating specific email messages
- Open the **Mail** app
- Click on the **search bar** at **top right** of window
- Next, type your **search query**
- If a dropdown display appears, select or click a **search option**

96

- You can decide to click on a **folder** to search
- Click the **email message** you want to open

Filtering email by unread
- Open Mail

- Click on **View** in menu bar at screen top left
- Click **Sort By**
- Click **Unread**

Marking an email as Unread

- Open **Mail**
- **Right-click** on the particular email you want to mark
- Click **Mark as Unread**

Deleting an email
- Open **mail**
- Click on the **email** you want to get rid of
- Click the **Delete button** at window top that appears as a dustbin

Chapter 15: Safari

Your Mac Air comes with a built in or pre-loaded web browser. It is called Safari. With safari, you can visit websites, bookmark your frequently visited pages and do a whole lot more.

Visiting a website

- Open **Safari** from the **Dock** or **Finder**
- Click the **address bar** at window top
- Type the **website address**
- Hit the **return** key to launch the search

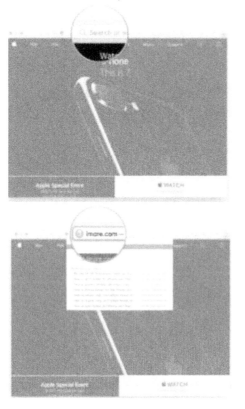

Searching with the address bar

- Open Safari
- Click the address bar at window top

100

- Next, type your **search Query**
- Tap **return** on your keyboard

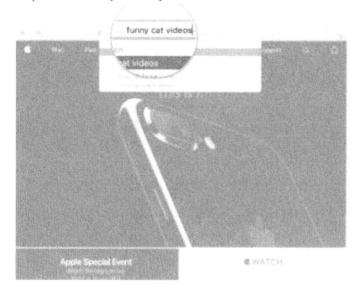

Bookmarking a website
- Open **safari**
- Open the **web page** you want to bookmark
- Press **Command-D** on your keyboard
- You can decide to type a title for the bookmark
- Click **Add** or tap **return** on your keyboard

- Click **View** in the menu bar at top left of screen
- Click **Show Favorites Bar**

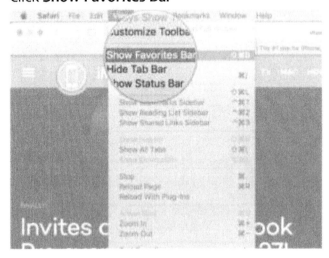

Viewing all bookmarks
- Open **Safari**
- Click the **Show sidebar button** beside the address bar
- Click the **bookmarks tab**

102

Removing Bookmarks

- Open **Safari**
- Click **Bookmarks** in **menu bar** at top left of the screen
- Click **Edit bookmarks**

- Click on the **arrow** beside **Favorites**
- **Right-click** or **control-click** the **bookmark** you want to delete
- Click **Delete**

Adding a web page to your reading list
- Open **Safari**
- Open the **website** you want to add
- Press **shift-command-D** on keyboard

Viewing your reading list
- Open **Safari**
- Click the **show sidebar button** close to the address bar
- Click the **reading list tab** represented by a pair of reading glasses
- Click the item you want to view

Deleting items from your reading list
- Open Safari
- Click show sidebar button next to the address bar
- Click the reading list tab

- **Right-click** or **control-click** the item you want to remove
- Click **Remove Item**

Enabling Private Browsing
- Open **Safari**
- Click **File** in the **menu bar** at screen top left
- Click **New Private Window**

Pinning Tabs
- Launch **Safari**
- Click View in **menu bar**
- Click **Show Tab Bar**
- Open the **website** you want to pin
- Click and hold the **tab** and **drag left**

Setting the homepage
- Open **Safari** from **Dock** or **Finder**
- Click **Safari** in **menu bar** from screen top left
- Next, click the **General tab**
- Enter a **website** next to **Homepage.** If you want the web Page to be your default homepage, you can also click **Set to Current Page**

107

- Click the **dropdown menu** next to **New windows open with**
- If you prefer new windows to be launched from your homepage, click **Homepage**
- Next, click the **dropdown menu** next to **New tabs open with**
- If you prefer new tabs to be launched to your homepage, click **Homepage**

108

Sharing websites
- Open **Safari**
- Open or launch the **website** to be shared
- From top right of Safari window, click the **Share Sheet button**
- Select a **sharing method**

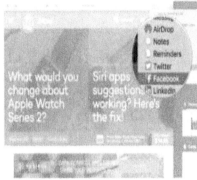

Customizing Favorites in Safari
- Open the **website** to be added as a favorite in Safari
- Move the **pointer** over the Smart Search field
- Click **Favorites**
- To remove or delete a website from your favorites list, click **Bookmarks** in the **Safari Toolbar**. Click **Show Favorites**. Right-click on the website to be removed. Click **Delete**

Organizing your Safari Favorites
- From the **Safari Toolbar,** click **Bookmarks**
- Click **Show Favorites**

109

- Move or drag your **favorite** to a new location on the list

Organizing your frequently visited sites in Safari
- From the **Safari Toolbar**, click **Bookmarks**
- Click **Show Favorites**
- Click **Show Frequently visited in Favorites** in same place

Deleting frequently visited sites
- From Safari, access the **Favorites** page
- Right-click the **website** you want to remove from under Frequently Visited
- Click **Delete**

Accessing Siri suggestions in Safari in macOS Catalina
- From the **Safari Toolbar**, click **Bookmarks**
- Click **Show Favorites**
- From under or within Siri suggestions, tap on a **link**

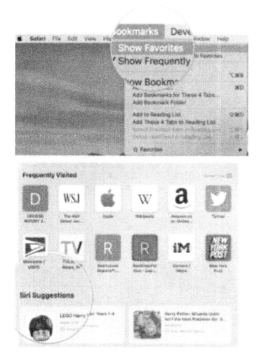

111

Chapter 16: Launch pad

If you have macOS Big Sur installed on your Mac Air, you have access to an iPad inspired home screen launcher and it allows you to do a host of stuff like, viewing, searching for, starting, managing and deleting apps on your Mac.

Opening apps via launchpad on your Mac
- You can select or opt for one of the following methods:
    1. Click the icon for **Launchpad** from the Dock
    2. On your **trackpad,** perform a **pinch gesture using four fingers**
    3. If you have a **Launchpad button** on your **Apple keyboard,** you can press it
- Next, click on the app you want to open

Locating apps via Launchpad
- Launch or access **Launchpad**
- Click the **search bar** at top center of Launchpad screen
- Enter **app name**
- Select the **app**

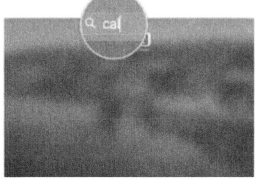

Moving apps around in Launchpad
- Launch or access **Launchpad**
- Click and hold a specific **app** till it starts jiggling
- Use your **mouse** to move the app

Sorting apps into folders
- Go to **Launchpad**
- Click and hold a specific **app** till it jiggles

113

- **Move or drag** the **app** on top of another app you want to put in the same folder till a white box shows around both apps
- Release the app to complete the process

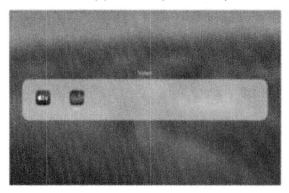

Deleting apps in Launchpad
- Access **Launchpad**
- Click and hold the **app** to be deleted till it jiggles
- Click the **X** on the app to delete it
- Click **Delete** in the pop-up box

Resetting Launchpad
- Click on **desktop**
- Click the **Go** menu in the menu bar at screen top
- Press and hold the **Option key**
- Click **Library**

- Click twice on the **Application support folder**
- Click twice on the **Dock folder**

- Next, move all files ending in **.db** to the bin
- Select the **Apple icon** at top left of screen
- Click **Restart**
- Confirm again with the **Restart button**

Chapter 17: Siri

The personal assistant that helps you out with most things is also here on your Mac but this time, it goes the extra mile and can do more than it was designed to do on other Apple devices. Just set it up and get it busy helping you out.

Enabling Siri on your Mac Air

- Click **Apple icon** at upper left corner of screen
- Click **System Preferences**

- Click **Siri**
- Check the box on the left side of the window to **Talk to Siri**

- Choose a **language**

- Choose a **Siri voice**

- Turn off **Voice Feedback** if you prefer Siri not to speak
- Choose a **Mic input** from the internal or external accessory

Activating "Type to Siri" (for macOS High Sierra)
- Click the **Apple menu** icon at screen upper left
- Click **System Preferences**

- Select **Accessibility**
- Click **Siri**
- Check or tick the box for **Enable Type to Siri**

117

Typing a query to Siri (macOS High Sierra)
- Click the **Apple menu** icon at upper left of screen
- Click **Preferences**
- Click **Accessibility**
- Click **Siri**
- Uncheck the box for **Enable Type to Siri**

Using a keyboard shortcut to enable Siri
- Click **Apple icon** at upper left screen corner
- Click **System Preferences** from dropdown menu
- Click **Siri**
- Choose a **keyboard shortcut** to use from under Keyboard shortcut

Using Siri with AirPods
- Click **Apple icon** at upper left of screen
- Choose **System Preferences**
- Click **Siri**
- Check the box for **Listen for "Hey Siri" on headphones**
- Check the box for **Allow Siri when locked**

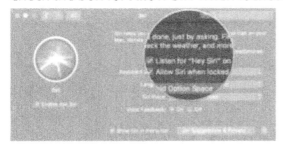

Pinning Siri results to notifications center
- Click on the **Siri icon** from the **Dock** or **Menu bar**
- Give Siri a **task** to execute
- When the search result shows in Siri's window, click the (+) button beside the search results

Chapter 18: Spotlight

Spotlight is basically a search engine that you can use to quickly and easily locate stuff on your Mac Air like photos, files, folders, documents etc.

Accessing and using Spotlight

- From the menu bar, click on the **Spotlight button**. you can alternatively use **Command + Space**
- Enter your **search query**
- Results would come into view as you type. To increase accuracy, you may want to adjust or specify your search terms to be more precise

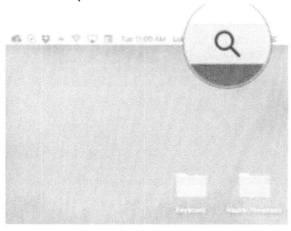

Customizing Spotlight search results

- Click **Apple menu** at top left of screen
- Select **System Preferences**
- Click **Spotlight**

- Click the **Checkbox** beside the category to alter or change what results Spotlight would display

Hiding content from Spotlight search
- Click the **Apple Menu** button at screen top left
- Select **System Preferences**
- Click **Spotlight**
- Click on the **Privacy tab**
- Click the add button represented by a + at bottom left of window

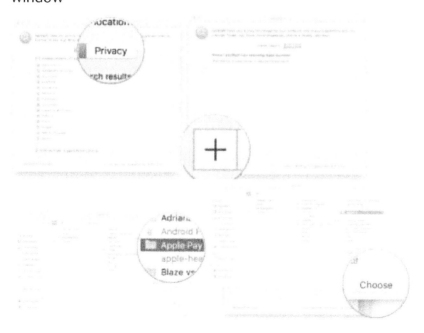

Chapter 20: Screenshots

If you ever feel the need to share an image you see on your Mac Air, the screen shot function is there to make it very possible for you to do so and very easily too.

Taking screen shots on your Mac Air

- To call up the screen shot toolbar, press **Command +Shift +5** on your keyboard
- Select from options such as **Capture Entire Screen**, **Capture Selected Windows** or **Capture Selected Portion**
- If you chose to capture anything other than your entire screen, click on your **Window or select screen portion**

- Next, Control-click, right-click or two -finger- click on the screenshot that shows at bottom right corner of the screen
- Decide the location to save the screenshot, send it, show it in the Finder, delete it etc

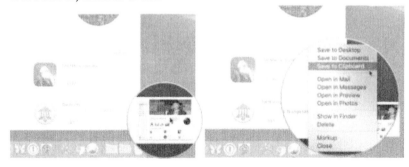

Doing a Screen recording

- Call up the screenshot toolbar via Command+Shift+5 on your keyboard

- Select **Record Entire Screen** or **Record Selected Portion**
- The recording should commence at once if you specified to record the entire screen. if you want to record a portion, specify the part of the screen

- Next, click **Record** on the screenshot and recording control bar
- When you are done, press the **Stop button** in the **menu bar** to end the recording

- Control-click, right-click or two-finger-click on the recording that would show at bottom right of the screen
- Use the **contextual menu** to decide the preferred location to save, send, show, delete or mark the screenshot

Choosing a save location for screenshots and screen recordings
- Use **Command+Shift+5** to call up the screenshot toolbar
- Select **Options**
- Choose from **Desktop, Documents, Clipboard, Mail, Messages** or **Preview** under save to specify a save location

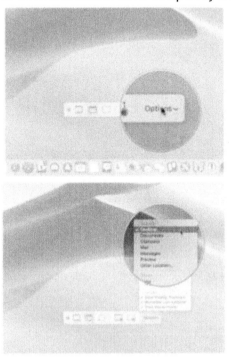

Setting a timer for screenshots and screen recordings
- Use **Command+Shift+5** to call up the screenshot toolbar
- Select **Options**

- Choose from **None, 5 seconds or 10 Seconds** under timer to set the timer

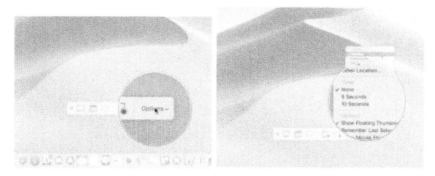

Showing the mouse pointer in screenshots
- Use **Command+Shift+5** to bring the screenshot toolbar in view
- Click **Options**
- Select **Show Mouse Pointer**

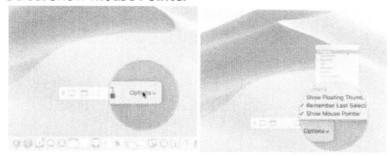

Editing a screenshot
- **Control-click, right-click, or two-finger-click** the screenshot that shows at bottom right corner of screen when you take a screenshot or do a screen recording
- Select **Markup**

125

- Use the **toolbar** at the top of quick look window to play do stuff like drawing, writing, to highlight, add shapes, insert text etc
- When you are satisfied, click **Done**

Editing a screen recording
- Repeat steps 1 and 2 as in editing a screenshot above
- Click the **trim button** close to the top-right corner of the **Quick Look window**
- Take hold of the hold points at each end of the recording's timeline and adjust their position to alter the length of the recording

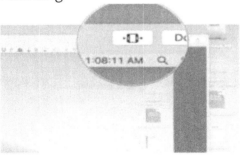

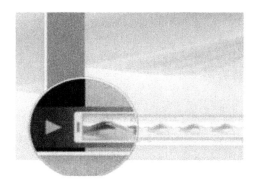

- Click **Done**

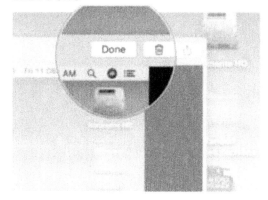

Chapter 21: Full screen mode

There may be times when you may need to zoom in on a specific app for better attention to detail. Find how to do so below:

Entering full screen mode
- From top left corner of the app window, select the **full-screen button.** you could also use the **Control+Command+F** keyboard shortcut

Navigating around full screen mode
- Place the **cursor** over the top of the screen to access the **menu bar**
- Move the **cursor** in the direction of the **Dock** to access the **Dock**
- Use a **three-finger swipe gesture** on the trackpad or use the **Command + Tab** shortcut keys to switch between apps while in full screen setting

Exiting full-screen mode
- Place the **cursor** over the top left corner and let the **window bar** show up. Click the red **Exit full-screen button**.
- To use the shortcut, press **control + Command + F**

Printed in Great Britain
by Amazon